*God Is in
the Manger*

DIETRICH BONHOEFFER

God Is in the Manger

Reflections on Advent and Christmas

TRANSLATED BY O. C. DEAN JR.

COMPILED AND EDITED BY JANA RIESS

WJK WESTMINSTER
JOHN KNOX PRESS
LOUISVILLE · KENTUCKY

© 2010 Westminster John Knox Press

First edition
Published by Westminster John Knox Press
Louisville, Kentucky

10 11 12 13 14 15 16 17 18 19—10 9 8 7 6 5 4 3 2 1

Scripture quotations from the New Revised Standard Version
of the Bible are copyright © 1989 by the Division of Christian Education of the
National Council of the Churches of Christ in the U.S.A. and are used by permission.

Scripture quotations from the Revised Standard Version of the Bible are
copyright © 1946, 1952, 1971, and 1973 by the Division of Christian Education of the
National Council of the Churches of Christ in the U.S.A. and are used by permission.

Devotional text herein originally appeared in
Dietrich Bonhoeffer's *I Want to Live These Days with You: A Year of Daily Devotions*
(Louisville, KY: Westminster John Knox Press, 2007).

Book design by Drew Stevens
Cover design by designpointinc.com

Library of Congress Cataloging-in-Publication Data

Bonhoeffer, Dietrich, 1906–1945.
  [Selections. English. 2010]
  God is in the manger : reflections on Advent and Christmas / by Dietrich
Bonhoeffer ; translated by O. C. Dean Jr. ; compiled and edited by Jana Riess.
  —1st ed.
    p. cm.
  Includes bibliographical references and index.
  ISBN 978-0-664-23429-4 (alk. paper)
  1. Advent—Meditations. 2. Christmas—Meditations I. Riess, Jana. II. Title.
BV40.B66513 2010
242'.33—dc22

2010003667

PRINTED IN THE UNITED STATES OF AMERICA

CONTENTS

⁓⁓⁓

Since Dietrich Bonhoeffer wrote before the days of inclusive gender, his works reflect a male-oriented world in which, for example, the German words for "human being" and "God" are masculine, and male gender was understood as common gender. In this respect, his language has, for the most part, been updated in accordance with the practices of the New Revised Standard Version of the Bible (NRSV); that is, most references to human beings have become gender-inclusive, whereas references to the Deity have remained masculine.

While scriptural quotations are mostly from the NRSV, it was necessary at times to substitute the King James Version (KJV), the Revised Standard Version (RSV), or a literal translation of Luther's German version, as quoted by Bonhoeffer, in order to allow the author to make his point. In a few other cases, the translation was adjusted to reflect the wording of the NRSV.

O. C. Dean Jr.

EDITOR'S PREFACE

This devotional brings together daily reflections from one of the twentieth century's most beloved theologians, Dietrich Bonhoeffer (1906–1945). These reflections have been chosen especially for the seasons of Advent and Christmas, a time when the liturgical calendar highlights several themes of Bonhoeffer's beliefs and teachings: that Christ expresses strength best through weakness, that faith is more important than the beguiling trappings of religion, and that God is often heard most clearly by those in poverty and distress.[1]

Although he came from a well-to-do family, by the time he wrote most of the content in this book, Bonhoeffer was well acquainted with both poverty and distress. Just two days after Adolf Hitler had seized control of Germany in early 1933, Bonhoeffer delivered a radio sermon in which he criticized the new regime and warned Germans that "the Führer concept" was dangerous and wrong. "Leaders of offices which set themselves up as gods mock God," his address concluded. But Germany never got to hear those final statements, because Bonhoeffer's microphone had been switched off mid-transmission.[2] This began a twelve-year struggle against Nazism in Germany, with Bonhoeffer running afoul of authorities and being arrested in 1943. Much of the content of this book was written during the two years he spent in prison.

For Bonhoeffer, waiting—one of the central themes of the Advent experience—was a fact of life during the war: waiting to be released from prison; waiting to be able to spend more than an hour a month in the company of his young fiancée, Maria von Wedemeyer; waiting for the end of the war. In his absence, friends and former students were killed in battle and his parents' home was bombed; there was little he could do about any of this except pray and wield a powerful pen. There was a helplessness in his situation that he recognized as a parallel to Advent, Christians' time of waiting for redemption in Christ. "Life in a prison cell may well be compared to Advent," Bonhoeffer wrote his best friend Eberhard Bethge as the holidays approached in 1943. "One waits, hopes, and does this, that, or the other—things that are really of no consequence—the door is shut, and can only be opened *from the outside*."[3]

But the prison door was never opened for Bonhoeffer, not in life at least. As the Third Reich crumbled in April 1945, Hitler ordered the execution of some political prisoners who had conspired to overthrow him. Since papers had recently been discovered that confirmed Bonhoeffer's involvement in this anti-Nazi plot, the theologian was among those scheduled to be executed in one of Hitler's final executive decrees.[4] Bonhoeffer was hanged on April 8, 1945, just ten days before German forces began to surrender and less than three weeks before Hitler's own death by suicide. Bonhoeffer was just thirty-nine years old.

Although Bonhoeffer's death (and the narrow timing of it) is tragic, we are fortunate that he was a prolific writer who left behind so many lectures, papers, letters, and diary entries from which we may piece together his theology.

HOW TO USE THIS BOOK

Advent is rarely exactly four weeks long, and can in fact vary in length from year to year. It always begins four Sundays before Christmas (December 25), but since Christmas falls on a different day of the week each year, Advent can begin anywhere between November 27 on the early side and December 3 on the late side. The first four weeks of this devotional assume the earliest possible start date, so that if Advent falls on or around November 27, you will have four full weeks of devotions to see you through to Christmas Day. If you're using the book in a year when Advent is slightly shorter, feel free to skip a few devotions in the first or last week.

The four Advent weeks are arranged by theme — waiting, mystery, redemption, and incarnation — and are followed by devotions for the twelve days of Christmas, which stretch from Christmas Day until January 5, just before the liturgical feast of Epiphany. These last entries are dated, since the twelve days of Christmas always begin on December 25 and end on January 5, unlike the varying days of Advent. This book also includes a final reflection for January 6, the feast of Epiphany.

Each day's devotion has a reflection from Dietrich Bonhoeffer, a Scripture to contemplate, and some bonus material. Most of the latter material is drawn from Bonhoeffer's own letters, sermons, and poetry, showing how he celebrated Christmas even when imprisoned and separated from family and beloved friends. It's important to remember how Bonhoeffer's beliefs were forged in the crucible of war and protest, and did not simply fall from the sky; it's equally important to recognize how intimately connected he was to those he loved. He did not exist in a vacuum. His legacy has also been profound, so a few of the bonus entries are taken from thinkers who might be called "heirs of Bonhoeffer"—contemporary Christian writers like Eugene Peterson, Luci Shaw, and Frederica Mathewes-Green, who reflect on some of the same issues that he did.

WAITING

～⌒～⌒～

The Advent Season Is a Season of Waiting

Jesus stands at the door knocking (Rev. 3:20). In total reality, he comes in the form of the beggar, of the dissolute human child in ragged clothes, asking for help. He confronts you in every person that you meet. As long as there are people, Christ will walk the earth as your neighbor, as the one through whom God calls you, speaks to you, makes demands on you. That is the great seriousness and great blessedness of the Advent message. Christ is standing at the door; he lives in the form of a human being among us. Do you want to close the door or open it?

It may strike us as strange to see Christ in such a near face, but he said it, and those who withdraw from the serious reality of the Advent message cannot talk of the coming of Christ in their heart, either. . . .

Christ is knocking. It's still not Christmas, but it's also still not the great last Advent, the last coming of Christ. Through all the Advents of our life that we celebrate runs the longing for the last Advent, when the word will be: "See, I am making all things new" (Rev. 21:5).

The Advent season is a season of waiting, but our whole life is an Advent season, that is, a season of waiting for the last Advent, for the time when there will be a new heaven and a new earth.

❖   ❖   ❖

We can, and should also, celebrate Christmas despite the ruins around us. . . . I think of you as you now sit together with the children and with all the Advent decorations — as in earlier years you did with us. We must do all this, even more intensively because we do not know how much longer we have.[1]

Letter to Bonhoeffer's parents, November 29, 1943,
written from Tegel prison camp

❖   ❖   ❖

Listen! I am standing at the door, knocking; if you hear my voice and open the door, I will come in to you and eat with you, and you with me.

Revelation 3:20

∞ ∞

Waiting Is an Art

Celebrating Advent means being able to wait. Waiting is an art that our impatient age has forgotten. It wants to break open the ripe fruit when it has hardly finished planting the shoot. But all too often the greedy eyes are only deceived; the fruit that seemed so precious is still green on the inside, and disrespectful hands ungratefully toss aside what has so disappointed them. Whoever does not know the austere blessedness of waiting—that is, of hopefully doing without—will never experience the full blessing of fulfillment.

Those who do not know how it feels to struggle anxiously with the deepest questions of life, of their life, and to patiently look forward with anticipation until the truth is revealed, cannot even dream of the splendor of the moment in which clarity is illuminated for them. And for those who do not want to win the friendship and love of another person—who do not expectantly open up their soul to the soul of the other person, until friendship and love come, until they make their entrance—for such people the deepest blessing of the one life of two intertwined souls will remain forever hidden.

For the greatest, most profound, tenderest things in the world, we must wait. It happens not here in a storm but according to the divine laws of sprouting, growing, and becoming.

Be brave for my sake, dearest Maria, even if this letter is your only token of my love this Christmas-tide. We shall both experience a few dark hours — why should we disguise that from each other? We shall ponder the incomprehensibility of our lot and be assailed by the question of why, over and above the darkness already enshrouding humanity, we should be subjected to the bitter anguish of a separation whose purpose we fail to understand. . . . And then, just when everything is bearing down on us to such an extent that we can scarcely withstand it, the Christmas message comes to tell us that all our ideas are wrong, and that what we take to be evil and dark is really good and light because it comes from God. Our eyes are at fault, that is all. God is in the manger, wealth in poverty, light in darkness, succor in abandonment. No evil can befall us; whatever men may do to us, they cannot but serve the God who is secretly revealed as love and rules the world and our lives.[2]

Letter to fiancée Maria von Wedemeyer
from prison, December 13, 1943

❖   ❖   ❖

A shoot shall come out from the stump of Jesse,
    and a branch shall grow out of his roots.
The spirit of the LORD shall rest on him,
    the spirit of wisdom and understanding,
    the spirit of counsel and might,
    the spirit of knowledge and the fear of the LORD.
His delight shall be in the fear of the LORD.

He shall not judge by what his eyes see,
    or decide by what his ears hear;
but with righteousness he shall judge the poor.

Isaiah 11:1–4a

Not Everyone Can Wait

Not everyone can wait: neither the sated nor the satisfied nor those without respect can wait. The only ones who can wait are people who carry restlessness around with them and people who look up with reverence to the greatest in the world. Thus Advent can be celebrated only by those whose souls give them no peace, who know that they are poor and incomplete, and who sense something of the greatness that is supposed to come, before which they can only bow in humble timidity, waiting until he inclines himself toward us—the Holy One himself, God in the child in the manger. God is coming; the Lord Jesus is coming; Christmas is coming. Rejoice, O Christendom!

❖   ❖   ❖

I think we're going to have an exceptionally good Christmas. The very fact that every outward circumstance precludes our making provision for it will show whether we can be content with what is truly essential. I used to be very fond of thinking up and buying presents, but now that we have nothing to give, the gift God gave us in the birth of Christ will seem all the more glorious; the emptier our hands, the better we understand what Luther meant by his dying words: "We're beggars; it's true." The poorer our quarters, the more clearly we perceive that our hearts should be Christ's home on earth.[3]

Letter to fiancée Maria von Wedemeyer,
December 1, 1943

❖   ❖   ❖

Then he looked up at his disciples and said:
"Blessed are you who are poor,
   for yours is the kingdom of God.
"Blessed are you who are hungry now,
   for you will be filled.
"Blessed are you who weep now,
   for you will laugh.
"Blessed are you when people hate you, and
when they exclude you, revile you, and defame you
on account of the Son of Man. Rejoice in that day
and leap for joy, for surely your reward is great in
heaven; for that is what their ancestors did to the
prophets.
"But woe to you who are rich,
   for you have received your consolation.
"Woe to you who are full now,
   for you will be hungry.
"Woe to you who are laughing now,
   for you will mourn and weep.
"Woe to you when all speak well of you, for that
is what their ancestors did to the false prophets."

Luke 6:20–26

ʘ⊃ ʘ⊃

An Un-Christmas-Like Idea

When the old Christendom spoke of the coming again of the Lord Jesus, it always thought first of all of a great day of judgment. And as un-Christmas-like as this idea may appear to us, it comes from early Christianity and must be taken with utter seriousness. . . . The coming of God is truly not only a joyous message, but is, first, frightful news for anyone who has a conscience. And only when we have felt the frightfulness of the matter can we know the incomparable favor. God comes in the midst of evil, in the midst of death, and judges the evil in us and in the world. And in judging it, he loves us, he purifies us, he sanctifies us, he comes to us with his grace and love. He makes us happy as only children can be happy.

❖   ❖   ❖

We have become so accustomed to the idea of divine love and of God's coming at Christmas that we no longer feel the shiver of fear that God's coming should arouse in us. We are indifferent to the message, taking only the pleasant and agreeable out of it and forgetting the serious aspect, that the God of the world draws near to the people of our little earth and lays claim to us.[4]

Dietrich Bonhoeffer, "The Coming
of Jesus in Our Midst"

In that region there were shepherds living in the fields, keeping watch over their flock by night. Then an angel of the Lord stood before them, and the glory of the Lord shone around them, and they were terrified. But the angel said to them, "Do not be afraid; for see — I am bringing you good news of great joy for all the people: to you is born this day in the city of David a Savior, who is the Messiah, the Lord. This will be a sign for you: you will find a child wrapped in bands of cloth and lying in a manger." And suddenly there was with the angel a multitude of the heavenly host, praising God and saying,

> "Glory to God in the highest heaven,
>   and on earth peace among those whom
>   he favors!"

Luke 2:8–14

∽∞∽

A Soft, Mysterious Voice

In the midst of the deepest guilt and distress of the people, a voice speaks that is soft and mysterious but full of the blessed certainty of salvation through the birth of a divine child (Isa. 9:6–7). It is still seven hundred years until the time of fulfillment, but the prophet is so deeply immersed in God's thought and counsel that he speaks of the future as if he saw it already, and he speaks of the salvific hour as if he already stood in adoration before the manger of Jesus. "For a child has been born for us." What will happen one day is already real and certain in God's eyes, and it will be not only for the salvation of future generations but already for the prophet who sees it coming and for his generation, indeed, for all generations on earth. "For a child has been born *for us*." No human spirit can talk like this on its own. How are we who do not know what will happen next year supposed to understand that someone can look forward many centuries? And the times then were no more transparent than they are today. Only the Spirit of God, who encompasses the beginning and end of the world, can in such a way reveal to a chosen person the mystery of the future, so that he must prophesy for strengthening believers and warning unbelievers. This individual voice ultimately enters into the nocturnal adoration of the shepherds (Luke 2:15–20) and into the full jubilation of the Christ-believing community: "For a child has been born for us, a son given to us."

❖ ❖ ❖

A shaking of heads, perhaps even an evil laugh, must go
through our old, smart, experienced, self-assured world,
when it hears the call of salvation of believing Christians:
"For a child has been born for us, a son given to us."[5]

Dietrich Bonhoeffer

❖ ❖ ❖

For a child has been born for us,
    a son given to us;
authority rests upon his shoulders;
    and he is named
Wonderful Counselor, Mighty God,
    Everlasting Father, Prince of Peace.
His authority shall grow continually,
    and there shall be endless peace
for the throne of David and his kingdom.
    He will establish and uphold it
with justice and with righteousness
    from this time onward and forevermore.
The zeal of the LORD of hosts will do this.

Isaiah 9:6–7

Silence: Waiting for God's Word

We are silent in the early hours of each day, because God is supposed to have the first word, and we are silent before going to sleep, because to God also belongs the last word. We are silent solely for the sake of the word, not in order to show dishonor to the word but in order to honor and receive it properly. Silence ultimately means nothing but waiting for God's word and coming away blessed by God's word. . . . Silence before the word, however, will have its effect on the whole day. If we have learned to be silent before the word, we will also learn to be economical with silence and speech throughout the day. There is an impermissible self-satisfied, prideful, offensive silence. This teaches us that what is important is never silence in itself. The silence of the Christian is a listening silence, a humble silence that for the sake of humility can also be broken at any time. It is a silence in connection with the word. . . . In being quiet there is a miraculous power of clarification, of purification, of bringing together what is important. This is a purely profane fact. Silence before the word, however, leads to the right hearing and thus also to the right speaking of the word of God at the right time. A lot that is unnecessary remains unsaid.

❖   ❖   ❖

Today is Remembrance Sunday. Will you have a memorial service for B. Riemer? It would be nice, but difficult. Then comes Advent, with all its happy memories for us. It was you who really opened up to me the world of music-making that we have carried on during the weeks of Advent. Life in a prison cell may well be compared to Advent: one waits, hopes, and does this, that, or the other—things that are really of no consequence—the door is shut, and can only be opened *from the outside.*[6]

Letter from Bonhoeffer at Tegel prison to
Eberhard Bethge, November 21, 1943

❖ ❖ ❖

For God alone my soul waits in silence,
    for my hope is from him.
He alone is my rock and my salvation,
    my fortress; I shall not be shaken.
On God rests my deliverance and my honor;
    my mighty rock, my refuge is in God.
Trust in him at all times, O people;
    pour out your heart before him;
    God is a refuge for us.

Psalm 62:5–8

God's Holy Present

Serve the opportune time." The most profound matter will be revealed to us only when we consider that not only does the world have its time and its hours, but also that our own life has its time and its hour of God, and that behind these times of our lives traces of God become visible, that under our paths are the deepest shafts of eternity, and every step brings back a quiet echo from eternity. It is only a matter of understanding the deep, pure form of these times and representing them in our conduct of life. Then in the middle of our time we will also encounter God's holy present. "My times are in your hand" (Ps. 31:15). Serve your times, God's present in your life. God has sanctified your time. Every time, rightly understood, is immediate to God, and God wants us to be fully what we are. . . . Only those who stand with both feet on the earth, who are and remain totally children of earth, who undertake no hopeless attempts at flight to unreachable heights, who are content with what they have and hold on to it thankfully—only they have the full power of the humanity that serves the opportune time and thus eternity. . . . The Lord of the ages is God. The turning point of the ages is Christ. The right spirit of the ages is the Holy Spirit.

❖　❖　❖

Dear parents . . . I don't need to tell you how much I long for freedom and for you all. But over the decades you have provided for us such incomparably beautiful Christmases that my thankful remembrance of them is strong enough to light up one dark Christmas. Only such times can really reveal what it means to have a past and an inner heritage that is independent of chance and the changing of the times. The awareness of a spiritual tradition that reaches through the centuries gives one a certain feeling of security in the face of all transitory difficulties. I believe that those who know they possess such reserves of strength do not need to be ashamed even of softer feelings—which in my opinion are still among the better and nobler feelings of humankind—when remembrance of a good and rich past calls them forth. Such feelings will not overwhelm those who hold fast to the values that no one can take from them.[7]

Letter to Bonhoeffer's parents, written from
Tegel prison, December 17, 1943

❖ ❖ ❖

For I hear the whispering of many—
    terror all around!—
as they scheme together against me,
    as they plot to take my life.

But I trust in you, O LORD;
    I say, "You are my God."
My times are in your hand;
    deliver me from the hand of my enemies
        and persecutors.
Let your face shine upon your servant;
    save me in your steadfast love.

Psalm 31:13–16

MYSTERY

Respect for the Mystery

The lack of mystery in our modern life is our downfall and our poverty. A human life is worth as much as the respect it holds for the mystery. We retain the child in us to the extent that we honor the mystery. Therefore, children have open, wide-awake eyes, because they know that they are surrounded by the mystery. They are not yet finished with this world; they still don't know how to struggle along and avoid the mystery, as we do. We destroy the mystery because we sense that here we reach the boundary of our being, because we want to be lord over everything and have it at our disposal, and that's just what we cannot do with the mystery. . . . Living without mystery means knowing nothing of the mystery of our own life, nothing of the mystery of another person, nothing of the mystery of the world; it means passing over our own hidden qualities and those of others and the world. It means remaining on the surface, taking the world seriously only to the extent that it can be *calculated* and *exploited*, and not going beyond the world of calculation and exploitation. Living without mystery means not seeing the crucial processes of life at all and even denying them.

❖   ❖   ❖

Ascension joy—inwardly we must become very quiet to hear the soft sound of this phrase at all. Joy lives in its quietness and incomprehensibility. This joy is in fact incomprehensible, for the comprehensible never makes for joy.[1]

Dietrich Bonhoeffer

❖   ❖   ❖

I want their hearts to be encouraged and united in love, so that they may have all the riches of assured understanding and have the knowledge of God's mystery, that is, Christ himself, in whom are hidden all the treasures of wisdom and knowledge.

Colossians 2:2–3

⌒⌒

The Mystery of Love

The mystery remains a mystery. It withdraws from our grasp. Mystery, however, does not mean simply not knowing something.

The greatest mystery is not the most distant star; on the contrary, the closer something comes to us and the better we know it, then the more mysterious it becomes for us. The greatest mystery to us is not the most distant person, but the one next to us. The mystery of other people is not reduced by getting to know more and more about them. Rather, in their closeness they become more and more mysterious. And the final depth of all mystery is when two people come so close to each other that they *love* each other. Nowhere in the world does one feel the might of the mysterious and its wonder as strongly as here. When two people know everything about each other, the mystery of the love between them becomes infinitely great. And only in this love do they understand each other, know everything about each other, know each other completely. And yet, the more they love each other and know about each other in love, the more deeply they know the mystery of their love. Thus, knowledge about each other does not remove the mystery, but rather makes it more profound. *The very fact* that the other person is so near to me is the greatest mystery.

❖　❖　❖

All that is Christmas originates in heaven and comes from there to us all, to you and me alike, and forms a stronger bond between us than we could ever forge by ourselves.[2]

Maria von Wedemeyer to Dietrich Bonhoeffer,
December 19, 1943, from Pätzig

❖ ❖ ❖

I thank my God every time I remember you, constantly praying with joy in every one of my prayers for all of you, because of your sharing in the gospel from the first day until now. I am confident of this, that the one who began a good work among you will bring it to completion by the day of Jesus Christ. It is right for me to think this way about all of you, because you hold me in your heart, for all of you share in God's grace with me, both in my imprisonment and in the defense and confirmation of the gospel. For God is my witness, how I long for all of you with the compassion of Christ Jesus. And this is my prayer, that your love may overflow more and more with knowledge and full insight to help you to determine what is best, so that in the day of Christ you may be pure and blameless, having produced the harvest of righteousness that comes through Jesus Christ for the glory and praise of God. I want you to know, beloved, that what has happened to me has actually helped to spread the gospel, so that it has become known throughout the whole imperial guard and to everyone else that my imprisonment is for Christ; and most of the brothers and sisters, having been made confident in the Lord by my imprisonment, dare to speak the word with greater boldness and without fear.

Philippians 1:3–14

The Wonder of All Wonders

God travels wonderful ways with human beings, but he does not comply with the views and opinions of people. God does not go the way that people want to prescribe for him; rather, his way is beyond all comprehension, free and self-determined beyond all proof.

Where reason is indignant, where our nature rebels, where our piety anxiously keeps us away: that is precisely where God loves to be. There he confounds the reason of the reasonable; there he aggravates our nature, our piety—that is where he wants to be, and no one can keep him from it. Only the humble believe him and rejoice that God is so free and so marvelous that he does wonders where people despair, that he takes what is little and lowly and makes it marvelous. And that is the wonder of all wonders, that God loves the lowly. . . . God is not ashamed of the lowliness of human beings. God marches right in. He chooses people as his instruments and performs his wonders where one would least expect them. God is near to lowliness; he loves the lost, the neglected, the unseemly, the excluded, the weak and broken.

❖　❖　❖

That . . . is the unrecognized mystery of this world: Jesus Christ. That this Jesus of Nazareth, the carpenter, was himself the Lord of glory: that was the mystery of God. It was a mystery because God became poor, low, lowly, and weak out of love for humankind, because God became a human being like us, so that we would become divine, and because he came to us so that we would come to him. God as the one who becomes low for our sakes, *God in Jesus of Nazareth — that is the secret, hidden wisdom* . . . that "no eye has seen nor ear heard nor the human heart conceived" (1 Cor. 2:9). . . . That is the *depth of the Deity,* whom *we worship as mystery* and *comprehend as mystery.*[3]

Dietrich Bonhoeffer

❖   ❖   ❖

None of the rulers of this age understood this; for if they had, they would not have crucified the Lord of glory. But, as it is written,

"What no eye has seen, nor ear heard,
    nor the human heart conceived,
what God has prepared for those who love
    him" —

these things God has revealed to us through the Spirit; for the Spirit searches everything, even the depths of God.

1 Corinthians 2:8–10

The Scandal of Pious People

The lowly God-man is the scandal of pious people and of people in general. This scandal is his historical ambiguity. The most incomprehensible thing for the pious is this man's claim that he is not only a pious human being but also the Son of God. Whence his authority: "But I say to you" (Matt. 5:22) and "Your sins are forgiven" (Matt. 9:2). If Jesus' nature had been deified, this claim would have been accepted. If he had given signs, as was demanded of him, they would have believed him. But at the point where it really mattered, he held back. And that created the scandal. Yet everything depends on this fact. If he had answered the Christ question addressed to him through a miracle, then the statement would no longer be true that he became a human being like us, for then there would have been an exception at the decisive point. . . . If Christ had documented himself with miracles, we would naturally believe, but then Christ would not be our salvation, for then there would not be faith in the God who became human, but only the recognition of an alleged supernatural fact. But that is not faith. . . . Only when I forgo visible proof, do I believe in God.

❖   ❖   ❖

The kingdom belongs to people who aren't tryin
good or impress anybody, even themselves. The
plotting how they can call attention to themselve
ing about how their actions will be interpreted or
ing if they will get gold stars for their behavior
centuries later, Jesus speaks pointedly to the
ascetic trapped in the fatal narcissism of spiritua
tionism, to those of us caught up in boasting abou
tories in the vineyard, to those of us fretting and
about our human weaknesses and character def
child doesn't have to struggle to get himself in a g
tion for having a relationship with God; he doesn'
craft ingenious ways of explaining his position to
doesn't have to create a pretty face for himself; h
have to achieve any state of spiritual feeling or in
understanding. All he has to do is happily accept t
ies, the gift of the kingdom.[4]

Brennan Manning, *The Ragamuf*

❖ ❖ ❖

But we proclaim Christ crucified, a stumblin
to Jews and foolishness to Gentiles, but t
who are the called, both Jews and Greeks
the power of God and the wisdom of God. F
foolishness is wiser than human wisdom, an
weakness is stronger than human strength.

1 Corinthian

❦❦

The Power and Glory of the Manger

For the great and powerful of this world, there are only two places in which their courage fails them, of which they are afraid deep down in their souls, from which they shy away. These are the manger and the cross of Jesus Christ. No powerful person dares to approach the manger, and this even includes King Herod. For this is where thrones shake, the mighty fall, the prominent perish, because God is with the lowly. Here the rich come to nothing, because God is with the poor and hungry, but the rich and satisfied he sends away empty. Before Mary, the maid, before the manger of Christ, before God in lowliness, the powerful come to naught; they have no right, no hope; they are judged. . . .

❖ ❖ ❖

Who among us will celebrate Christmas correctly? Whoever finally lays down all power, all honor, all reputation, all vanity, all arrogance, all individualism beside the manger; whoever remains lowly and lets God alone be high; whoever looks at the child in the manger and sees the glory of God precisely in his lowliness.[5]

Dietrich Bonhoeffer

❖ ❖ ❖

And Mary said,
"My soul magnifies the Lord,
    and my spirit rejoices in God my Savior,
for he has looked with favor on the lowliness of his
        servant.
    Surely, from now on all generations will call me
    blessed;
for the Mighty One has done great things for me,
    and holy is his name.
His mercy is for those who fear him
    from generation to generation.
He has shown strength with his arm;
    he has scattered the proud in the thoughts of
        their hearts.
He has brought down the powerful from their
        thrones,
    and lifted up the lowly;
he has filled the hungry with good things,
    and sent the rich away empty.
He has helped his servant Israel,
    in remembrance of his mercy,
    according to the promise he made to our
        ancestors,
    to Abraham and to his descendants forever."

Luke 1:46–55

⌒⌒⌒

The Mysteries of God

No priest, no theologian stood at the manger of Bethlehem. And yet all Christian theology has its origin in the wonder of all wonders: that God became human. Holy theology arises from knees bent before the mystery of the divine child in the stable. Without the holy night, there is no theology. "God is revealed in flesh," the God-human Jesus Christ — that is the holy mystery that theology came into being to protect and preserve. How we fail to understand when we think that the task of theology is to solve the mystery of God, to drag it down to the flat, ordinary wisdom of human experience and reason! Its sole office is to preserve the miracle as miracle, to comprehend, defend, and glorify God's mystery precisely as mystery. This and nothing else, therefore, is what the early church meant when, with never flagging zeal, it dealt with the mystery of the Trinity and the person of Jesus Christ. . . . If Christmas time cannot ignite within us again something like a love for holy theology, so that we — captured and compelled by the wonder of the manger of the Son of God — must reverently reflect on the mysteries of God, then it must be that the glow of the divine mysteries has also been extinguished in our heart and has died out.

❖   ❖   ❖

Wonder is the only adequate launching pad for exploring this fullness, this wholeness, of human life. Once a year, each Christmas, for a few days at least, we and millions of our neighbors turn aside from our preoccupations with life reduced to biology or economics or psychology and join together in a community of wonder. The wonder keeps us open-eyed, expectant, alive to life that is always more than we can account for, that always exceeds our calculations, that is always beyond anything we can make.[6]

Eugene Peterson

❖　❖　❖

When the angels had left them and gone into heaven, the shepherds said to one another, "Let us go now to Bethlehem and see this thing that has taken place, which the Lord has made known to us." So they went with haste and found Mary and Joseph, and the child lying in the manger. When they saw this, they made known what had been told them about this child; and all who heard it were amazed at what the shepherds told them. But Mary treasured all these words and pondered them in her heart. The shepherds returned, glorifying and praising God for all they had heard and seen, as it had been told them.

Luke 2:15–20

An Unfathomable Mystery

In an incomprehensible reversal of all righteous and pious thinking, God declares himself guilty to the world and thereby extinguishes the guilt of the world. God himself takes the humiliating path of reconciliation and thereby sets the world free. God wants to be guilty of our guilt and takes upon himself the punishment and suffering that this guilt brought to us. God stands in for godlessness, love stands in for hate, the Holy One for the sinner. Now there is no longer any godlessness, any hate, any sin that God has not taken upon himself, suffered, and atoned for. Now there is no more reality and no more world that is not reconciled with God and in peace. That is what God did in his beloved Son Jesus Christ. *Ecce homo* — see the incarnate God, the unfathomable mystery of the love of God for the world. God loves human beings. God loves the world — not ideal human beings but people as they are, not an ideal world but the real world.

❖ ❖ ❖

We prepare to witness a mystery. More to the point, we prepare to witness *the* Mystery, the *God made flesh.* While it is good that we seek to know the Holy One, it is probably not so good to presume that we ever complete the task, to suppose that we ever know anything about him except what he has *made known* to us. The prophet Isaiah helps us to remember our limitations when he writes, "To whom then will you compare me . . . ? says the Holy One. . . ." Think of it like this: he cannot be exhausted by our ideas about him, but he is everywhere suggested. He cannot be comprehended, but he can be touched. His coming in the flesh — this Mystery we prepare to glimpse again — confirms that he is to be touched.[7]

Scott Cairns, in God with Us

❖ ❖ ❖

To whom then will you liken God,
   or what likeness compare with him? . . .
. . . .
Have you not known? Have you not heard?
   Has it not been told you from the beginning?
   Have you not understood from the foundations of
      the earth?
It is he who sits above the circle of the earth,
   and its inhabitants are like grasshoppers;
who stretches out the heavens like a curtain,
   and spreads them like a tent to live in;
who brings princes to naught,
   and makes the rulers of the earth as nothing.

Isaiah 40:18, 21–23

REDEMPTION

DAY ONE

Jesus Enters into the
Guilt of Human Beings

Jesus does not want to be the only perfect human being at the expense of humankind. He does not want, as the only guiltless one, to ignore a humanity that is being destroyed by its guilt; he does not want some kind of human ideal to triumph over the ruins of a wrecked humanity. Love for real people leads into the fellowship of human guilt. Jesus does not want to exonerate himself from the guilt in which the people he loves are living. A love that left people alone in their guilt would not have real people as its object. So, in vicarious responsibility for people and in his love for real human beings, Jesus becomes the one burdened by guilt—indeed, the one upon whom all human guilt ultimately falls and the one who does not turn it away but bears it humbly and in eternal love. As the one who acts responsibly in the historical existence of humankind, as the human being who has entered reality, Jesus becomes guilty. But because his historical existence, his incarnation, has its sole basis in God's love for human beings, it is the love of God that makes Jesus become guilty. Out of selfless love for human beings, Jesus leaves his state as the one without sin and enters into the guilt of human beings. He takes it upon himself.

❖ ❖ ❖

We have something to hide. We have secrets, worries, thoughts, hopes, desires, passions which no one else gets to know. We are sensitive when people get near those domains with their questions. And now, against all rules of tact the Bible speaks of the truth that in the end we will appear before Christ with everything we are and were. . . . And we all know that we could justify ourselves before any human court, but not before this one. Lord, who can justify themselves?[1]

Bonhoeffer's sermon for Repentance
Sunday, November 19, 1933

❖   ❖   ❖

For all of us must appear before the judgment seat of Christ, so that each may receive recompense for what has been done in the body, whether good or evil.

2 Corinthians 5:10

Taking on Guilt

Because what is at stake for Jesus is not the proclamation and realization of new ethical ideals, and thus also not his own goodness (Matt. 19:17), but solely his love for real human beings, he can enter into the communication of their guilt; he can be loaded down with their guilt. . . . It is his love alone that lets him become guilty. Out of his selfless love, out of his sinless nature, Jesus enters into the guilt of human beings; he takes it upon himself. A sinless nature and guilt bearing are bound together in him indissolubly. As the sinless one Jesus takes guilt upon himself, and under the burden of this guilt, he shows that he is the sinless one.

❖   ❖   ❖

Lord Jesus, come yourself, and dwell with us, be human as we are, and overcome what overwhelms us. Come into the midst of my evil, come close to my unfaithfulness. Share my sin, which I hate and which I cannot leave. Be my brother, Thou Holy God. Be my brother in the kingdom of evil and suffering and death.[2]

Sermon for Advent Sunday,
December 2, 1928

❖　❖　❖

Then someone came to him and said, "Teacher, what good deed must I do to have eternal life?" And he said to him, "Why do you ask me about what is good? There is only one who is good. If you wish to enter into life, keep the commandments." He said to him, "Which ones?" And Jesus said, "You shall not murder; You shall not commit adultery; You shall not steal; You shall not bear false witness; Honor your father and mother; also, You shall love your neighbor as yourself."

Matthew 19:16–19

～～

Becoming Guilty

Because Jesus took upon himself the guilt of all people, everyone who acts responsibly becomes guilty. Those who want to extract themselves from the responsibility for this guilt, also remove themselves from the ultimate reality of human existence. Moreover, they also remove themselves from the redeeming mystery of the sinless guilt bearing of Jesus Christ and have no share in the divine justification that covers this event. They place their personal innocence above their responsibility for humankind, and they are blind to the unhealed guilt that they load on themselves in this very way. They are also blind to the fact that real innocence is revealed in the very fact that for the sake of other people it enters into the communion of their guilt. Through Jesus Christ, the nature of responsible action includes the idea that the sinless, the selflessly loving become the guilty.

❖ ❖ ❖

In eight days, we shall celebrate Christmas and now for once let us make it really a festival of Christ in our world. . . . It is not a light thing to God that every year we celebrate Christmas and do not take it seriously. His word holds and is certain. When he comes in his glory and power into the world in the manger, he will put down the mighty from their seats, unless ultimately, ultimately they repent.[3]

Sermon to a London church on the third
Sunday of Advent, December 17, 1933

❖ ❖ ❖

Come now, let us argue it out,
    says the LORD:
though your sins are like scarlet,
    they shall be like snow;
though they are red like crimson,
    they shall become like wool.

Isaiah 1:18

DAY FOUR

∽∽ ∽∽

Look Up, Your Redemption
Is Drawing Near

Let's not deceive ourselves. "Your redemption is drawing near" (Luke 21:28), whether we know it or not, and the only question is: Are we going to let it come to us too, or are we going to resist it? Are we going to join in this movement that comes down from heaven to earth, or are we going to close ourselves off? Christmas is coming—whether it is with us or without us depends on each and every one of us.

Such a true Advent happening now creates something different from the anxious, petty, depressed, feeble Christian spirit that we see again and again, and that again and again wants to make Christianity contemptible. This becomes clear from the two powerful commands that introduce our text: "Look up and raise your heads" (Luke 21:28 RSV). Advent creates people, new people. We too are supposed to become new people in Advent. Look up, you whose gaze is fixed on this earth, who are spellbound by the little events and changes on the face of the earth. Look up to these words, you who have turned away from heaven disappointed. Look up, you whose eyes are heavy with tears and who are heavy and who are crying over the fact that the earth has gracelessly torn us away. Look up, you who, burdened with guilt, cannot lift your eyes. Look up, your redemption is drawing near. Something different from what you see daily will happen. Just be aware, be watchful, wait

just another short moment. Wait and something quite
new will break over you: God will come.

❖ ❖ ❖

You know what a mine disaster is. In recent weeks we
have had to read about one in the newspapers.

The moment even the most courageous miner has
dreaded his whole life long is here. It is no use running
into the walls; the silence all around him remains. . . . The
way out for him is blocked. He knows the people up there
are working feverishly to reach the miners who are buried
alive. Perhaps someone will be rescued, but here in the last
shaft? An agonizing period of waiting and dying is all that
remains.

But suddenly a noise that sounds like tapping and
breaking in the rock can be heard. Unexpectedly, voices
cry out, "Where are you, help is on the way!" Then the
disheartened miner picks himself up, his heart leaps, he
shouts, "Here I am, come on through and help me! I'll hold
out until you come! Just come soon!" A final, desperate
hammer blow to his ear, now the rescue is near, just one
more step and he is free.

We have spoken of Advent itself. That is how it is with
the coming of Christ: "Look up and raise your heads,
because your redemption is drawing near."[4]

Bonhoeffer's Advent sermon in a London
church, December 3, 1933

❖ ❖ ❖

Now when these things begin to take place, stand
up and raise your heads, because your redemption is
drawing near.

Luke 21:28

─────── ⚭ ───────

World Judgment and World Redemption

When God chooses Mary as the means when God himself wants to come into the world in the manger of Bethlehem, this is not an idyllic family affair. It is instead the beginning of a complete reversal, a new ordering of all things on this earth. If we want to participate in this Advent and Christmas event, we cannot simply sit there like spectators in a theater and enjoy all the friendly pictures. Rather, we must join in the action that is taking place and be drawn into this reversal of all things ourselves. Here we too must act on the stage, for here the spectator is always a person acting in the drama. We cannot remove ourselves from the action.

With whom, then, are we acting? Pious shepherds who are on their knees? Kings who bring their gifts? What is going on here, where Mary becomes the mother of God, where God comes into the world in the lowliness of the manger? World judgment and world redemption—that is what's happening here. And it is the Christ child in the manger himself who holds world judgment and world redemption. He pushes back the high and mighty; he overturns the thrones of the powerful; he humbles the haughty; his arm exercises power over all the high and mighty; he lifts what is lowly, and makes it great and glorious in his mercy.

❖   ❖   ❖

Close to you I waken in the dead of night,
And start with fear—are you lost to me once more?
   Is it always vainly that I seek you, you, my past?
I stretch my hands out,
and I pray—
and a new thing now I hear;
"The past will come to you once more,
and be your life's enduring part,
through thanks and repentance.
Feel in the past God's deliverance and goodness,
Pray him to keep you today and tomorrow."[5]

                    Poem written in Tegel prison, 1944

❖   ❖   ❖

"For God so loved the world that he gave his only
Son, so that everyone who believes in him may not
perish but may have eternal life.

"Indeed, God did not send the Son into the world
to condemn the world, but in order that the world
might be saved through him. Those who believe in
him are not condemned; but those who do not believe
are condemned already, because they have not
believed in the name of the only Son of God. And
this is the judgment, that the light has come into the
world, and people loved darkness rather than light
because their deeds were evil. For all who do evil
hate the light and do not come to the light, so that
their deeds may not be exposed. But those who do
what is true come to the light, so that it may be clearly
seen that their deeds have been done in God."

                                      John 3:16–21

DAY SIX

Overcoming Fear

Human beings are dehumanized by fear. . . . But they should not be afraid. We should not be afraid! That is the difference between human beings and the rest of creation, that in all hopelessness, uncertainty, and guilt, they know a hope, and this hope is: Thy will be done. Yes. Thy will be done. . . . We call the name of the One before whom the evil in us cringes, before whom fear and anxiety must themselves be afraid, before whom they shake and take flight; the name of the One who alone conquered fear, captured it and led it away in a victory parade, nailed it to the cross and banished it to nothingness; the name of the One who is the victory cry of the humanity that is redeemed from the fear of death—Jesus Christ, the one who was crucified and lives. He alone is the Lord of fear; it knows him as its Lord and yields to him alone. Therefore, look to him in your fear. Think about him, place him before your eyes, and call him. Pray to him and believe that he is now with you and helps you. The fear will yield and fade, and you will become free through faith in the strong and living Savior Jesus Christ (Matt. 8:23–27).

❖　❖　❖

Only when we have felt the terror of the matter, can we recognize the incomparable kindness. God comes into the very midst of evil and death, and judges the evil in us and in the world. And by judging us, God cleanses and sanctifies us, comes to us with grace and love. . . . God wants to always be with us, wherever we may be—in our sin, suffering, and death. We are no longer alone; God is with us.[6]

"The Coming of Jesus in Our Midst"

❖ ❖ ❖

And when he got into the boat, his disciples followed him. A windstorm arose on the sea, so great that the boat was being swamped by the waves; but he was asleep. And they went and woke him up, saying, "Lord, save us! We are perishing!" And he said to them, "Why are you afraid, you of little faith?" Then he got up and rebuked the winds and the sea; and there was a dead calm. They were amazed, saying, "What sort of man is this, that even the winds and the sea obey him?"

Matthew 8:23–27

God Does Not Want to Frighten People

The Bible never wants to make us fearful. God does not want people to be afraid—not even of the last judgment. Rather, he wants to let human beings know everything, so that they will know all about life and its meaning. He lets people know even today, so that they may already live their lives openly and in the light of the last judgment. He lets us know solely for one reason: so that we may find the way to Jesus Christ, so that we may turn away from our evil way and try to find him, Jesus Christ. God does not want to frighten people. He sends us the word of judgment only so that we will reach all the more passionately, all the more avidly, for the promise of grace, so that we will know that we cannot prevail before God on our own strength, that before him we would have to pass away, but that in spite of everything he does not want our death, but our life. . . . Christ judges, that is, grace is judge and forgiveness and love—whoever clings to it is already set free.

❖　❖　❖

Repentance means turning away from one's own work to the mercy of God. The whole Bible calls to us and cheers us: Turn back, turn back! Return—where to? To the everlasting grace of God, who does not leave us. . . . God will be merciful—so come, judgment day! Lord Jesus, make us ready. We rejoice. Amen.[7]

Bonhoeffer's sermon for Repentance
Sunday, November 19, 1933

❖ ❖ ❖

From that time Jesus began to proclaim, "Repent, for the kingdom of heaven has come near."

Matthew 4:17

INCARNATION

∞ ∞

God Becomes Human

God becomes human, really human. While we endeavor to grow out of our humanity, to leave our human nature behind us, God becomes human, and we must recognize that God wants us also to become human—really human. Whereas we distinguish between the godly and the godless, the good and the evil, the noble and the common, God loves real human beings without distinction. . . . God takes the side of real human beings and the real world against all their accusers. . . . But it's not enough to say that God takes care of human beings. This sentence rests on something infinitely deeper and more impenetrable, namely, that in the conception and birth of Jesus Christ, God took on humanity in bodily fashion. God raised his love for human beings above every reproach of falsehood and doubt and uncertainty by himself entering into the life of human beings as a human being, by bodily taking upon himself and bearing the nature, essence, guilt, and suffering of human beings. Out of love for human beings, God becomes a human being. He does not seek out the most perfect human being in order to unite with that person. Rather, he takes on human nature as it is.

❖ ❖ ❖

This is about the birth of a child, not of the astonishing work of a strong man, not of the bold discovery of a wise man, not of the pious work of a saint. It really is beyond all our understanding: the birth of a child shall bring about the great change, shall bring to all mankind salvation and deliverance.[1]

"The Government upon the Shoulders
of a Child," Christmas 1940

❖ ❖ ❖

In the beginning was the Word, and the Word was with God, and the Word was God. He was in the beginning with God. All things came into being through him, and without him not one thing came into being. What has come into being in him was life, and the life was the light of all people. The light shines in the darkness, and the darkness did not overcome it.

John 1:1–5

Human Beings Become Human Because God Became Human

The figure of Jesus Christ takes shape in human beings. Human beings do not take on an independent form of their own. Rather, what gives them form and maintains them in their new form is always and only the figure of Jesus Christ himself. It is therefore not an imitation, not a repetition of his form, but their own form that takes shape in human beings. Human beings are not transformed into a form that is foreign to them, not into the form of God, but into their own form, a form that belongs to them and is essential to them. Human beings become human because God became human, but human beings do not become God. They could not and cannot bring about that change in their form, but God himself changes his form into human form, so that human beings—though not becoming God—can become human.

In Christ the form of human beings before God was created anew. It was not a matter of place, of time, of climate, of race, of the individual, of society, of religion, or of taste, but rather a question of the life of humanity itself that it recognized in Christ its image and its hope. What happened to Christ happened to humanity.

❖   ❖   ❖

The whole Christian story is strange. Frederick Buechner describes the Incarnation as "a kind of vast joke whereby the creator of the ends of the earth comes among us in diapers." He concludes, "Until we too have taken the idea of the God-man seriously enough to be scandalized by it, we have not taken it as seriously as it demands to be taken."

But we have taken the idea as seriously as a child can. America is far from spiritually monolithic, but the vast backdrop of our culture is Christian, and for most of us it is the earliest faith we know. The "idea of the God-man" is not strange or scandalous, because it first swam in milk and butter on the top of our oatmeal decades ago. At that age, many things were strange, though most were more immediately palpable. A God-filled baby in a pile of straw was a pleasant image, but somewhat theoretical compared with the heart-stopping exhilaration of a visit from Santa Claus. The way a thunderstorm ripped the night sky, the hurtling power of the automobile Daddy drove so bravely, the rapture of ice cream — how could the distant Incarnation compete with those?

We grew up with the Jesus story, until we outgrew it. The last day we walked out of Sunday School may be the last day we seriously engaged this faith.[2]

Frederica Mathewes-Green,
At the Corner of East and Now

❖ ❖ ❖

When I was a child, I spoke like a child, I thought like a child, I reasoned like a child; when I became an adult, I put an end to childish ways. For now we see in a mirror, dimly, but then we will see face to face. Now I know only in part; then I will know fully, even as I have been fully known.

1 Corinthians 13:11–12

⚭ ⚭

Christmas, Fulfilled Promise

Moses died on the mountain from which he was permitted to view from a distance the promised land (Deut. 32:48–52). When the Bible speaks of God's promises, it's a matter of life and death. . . . The language that reports this ancient history is clear. Anyone who has seen God must die; the sinner dies before the promise of God. Let's understand what that means for us so close to Christmas. The great promise of God—a promise that is infinitely more important than the promise of the promised land—is supposed to be fulfilled at Christmas. . . . The Bible is full of the proclamation that the great miracle has happened as an act of God, without any human doing. . . . What happened? God had seen the misery of the world and had come himself in order to help. Now he was there, not as a mighty one, but in the obscurity of humanity, where there is sinfulness, weakness, wretchedness, and misery in the world. That is where God goes, and there he lets himself be found by everyone. And this proclamation moves through the world anew, year after year, and again this year also comes to us.

❖   ❖   ❖

We all come with different personal feelings to the Christmas festival. One comes with pure joy as he looks forward to this day of rejoicing, of friendships renewed, and of love. . . . Others look for a moment of peace under the

Christmas tree, peace from the pressures of daily work. . . .
Others again approach Christmas with great apprehen-
sion. It will be no festival of joy to them. Personal sorrow is
painful especially on this day for those whose loneliness is
deepened at Christmastime. . . . And despite it all, Christmas comes. Whether we wish it or not, whether we are
sure or not, we must hear the words once again: Christ the
Savior is here! The world that Christ comes to save is our
fallen and lost world. None other.[3]

Sermon to a German-speaking church in
Havana, Cuba, December 21, 1930

❖ ❖ ❖

In the sixth month the angel Gabriel was sent by
God to a town in Galilee called Nazareth, to a virgin
engaged to a man whose name was Joseph, of the
house of David. The virgin's name was Mary. And he
came to her and said, "Greetings, favored one! The
Lord is with you." But she was much perplexed by
his words and pondered what sort of greeting this
might be. The angel said to her, "Do not be afraid,
Mary, for you have found favor with God. And now,
you will conceive in your womb and bear a son, and
you will name him Jesus. He will be great, and will
be called the Son of the Most High, and the Lord
God will give to him the throne of his ancestor David.
He will reign over the house of Jacob forever, and of
his kingdom there will be no end."

Luke 1:26–33

The Great Turning Point of All Things

What kings and leaders of nations, philosophers and artists, founders of religions and teachers of morals have tried in vain to do—that now happens through a newborn child. Putting to shame the most powerful human efforts and accomplishments, a child is placed here at the midpoint of world history—a child born of human beings, a son given by God (Isa. 9:6). That is the mystery of the redemption of the world; everything past and everything future is encompassed here. The infinite mercy of the almighty God comes to us, descends to us in the form of a child, his Son. That this child is born *for us*, this son is given *to us*, that this human child and Son of God belongs to me, that I know him, have him, love him, that I am his and he is mine—on this alone my life now depends. A child has our life in his hands. . . .

❖ ❖ ❖

How shall we deal with such a child? Have our hands, soiled with daily toil, become too hard and too proud to fold in prayer at the sight of this child? Has our head become too full of serious thoughts . . . that we cannot bow our head in humility at the wonder of this child? Can we not forget all our stress and struggles, our sense of importance, and for once worship the child, as did the shepherds and the wise men from the East, bowing before the divine child in the manger like children?[4]

"The Government upon the Shoulders of the Child," Christmas 1940

❖ ❖ ❖

What then are we to say about these things? If God is for us, who is against us? He who did not withhold his own Son, but gave him up for all of us, will he not with him also give us everything else? Who will bring any charge against God's elect? It is God who justifies. Who is to condemn? It is Christ Jesus, who died, yes, who was raised, who is at the right hand of God, who indeed intercedes for us.

Romans 8:31–34

God Became a Child

Mighty God" (Isa. 9:6) is the name of this child. The child in the manger is none other than God himself. Nothing greater can be said: God became a child. In the Jesus child of Mary lives the almighty God. Wait a minute! Don't speak; stop thinking! Stand still before this statement! God became a child! Here he is, poor like us, miserable and helpless like us, a person of flesh and blood like us, our brother. And yet he is God; he is might. Where is the divinity, where is the might of the child? In the divine love in which he became like us. His poverty in the manger is his might. In the might of love he overcomes the chasm between God and humankind, he overcomes sin and death, he forgives sin and awakens from the dead. Kneel down before this miserable manger, before this child of poor people, and repeat in faith the stammering words of the prophet: "Mighty God!" And he will be your God and your might.

❖   ❖   ❖

But now it is true that in three days, Christmas will come once again. The great transformation will once again happen. God would have it so. Out of the waiting, hoping, longing world, a world will come in which the promise is given. All crying will be stilled. No tears shall flow. No lonely sorrow shall afflict us anymore, or threaten.[5]

> Sermon to a German-speaking church in
> Havana, Cuba, December 21, 1930

❖   ❖   ❖

And the Word became flesh and lived among us, and we have seen his glory, the glory as of a father's only son, full of grace and truth.

John 1:14

The Unfathomably Wise Counselor

Wonderful Counselor" (Isa. 9:6) is the name of this child. In him the wonder of all wonders has taken place; the birth of the Savior-child has gone forth from God's eternal counsel. In the form of a human child, God gave us his Son; God became human, the Word became flesh (John 1:14). That is the wonder of the love of God for us, and it is the unfathomably wise Counselor who wins us this love and saves us. But because this child of God is his own Wonderful Counselor, he himself is also the source of all wonder and all counsel. To those who recognize in Jesus the wonder of the Son of God, every one of his words and deeds becomes a wonder; they find in him the last, most profound, most helpful counsel for all needs and questions. Yes, before the child can open his lips, he is full of wonder and full of counsel. Go to the child in the manger. Believe him to be the Son of God, and you will find in him wonder upon wonder, counsel upon counsel.

❖   ❖   ❖

In winter it seems that the season of Spring will never come, and in both Advent and Lent it's the waiting that's hard, the in-between of divine promise and its fulfillment. . . . Most of us find ourselves dangling in this hiatus, which in the interval may seem a waste of time. . . . But "the longer we wait, the larger we become, and the more joyful our expectancy." With such motivation, we can wait as we sense that God is indeed *with us*, and at work within us, as he was with Mary as the Child within her grew.[6]

Poet Luci Shaw, in *God with Us*

❖ ❖ ❖

But when the fullness of time had come, God sent his Son, born of a woman, born under the law, in order to redeem those who were under the law, so that we might receive adoption as children. And because you are children, God has sent the Spirit of his Son into our hearts, crying, "Abba! Father!" So you are no longer a slave but a child, and if a child then also an heir, through God.

Galatians 4:4–7

~ ∞ ∞ ~

The One Who Became Human

Who is this God? This God is the one who became human as we became human. He is completely human. Therefore, nothing human is foreign to him. The human being that I am, Jesus Christ was also. About this human being Jesus Christ we say: this one is God. This does not mean that we already knew beforehand who God is. Nor does it mean that the statement "this human being is God" adds anything to being human. God and human being are not thought of as belonging together through a concept of nature. The statement "this human being is God" is meant entirely differently. The divinity of this human being is not something additional to the human nature of Jesus Christ. The statement "this human being is God" *is the vertical from above*, the statement that applies to Jesus Christ the human being, which neither adds anything nor takes anything away, but qualifies the whole human being as God. . . . Faith is ignited from Jesus Christ the human being. . . . If Jesus Christ is to be described as God, then we do not speak of his omnipotence and omniscience, but of his cradle and his cross. There is no "divine being" as omnipotence, as omnipresence.

❖   ❖   ❖

And now Christmas is coming and you won't be there. We shall be apart, yes, but very close together. My thoughts will come to you and accompany you. We shall sing "Friede auf Erden" [Peace on Earth] and pray together, but we shall sing "Ehre sei Gott in der Höhe!" [Glory be to God on high] even louder. That is what I pray for you and for all of us, that the Savior may throw open the gates of heaven for us at darkest night on Christmas Eve, so that we can be joyful in spite of everything.[7]

Maria von Wedemeyer to Bonhoeffer,
December 10, 1943

❖　❖　❖

In those days a decree went out from Emperor Augustus that all the world should be registered. This was the first registration and was taken while Quirinius was governor of Syria. All went to their own towns to be registered. Joseph also went from the town of Nazareth in Galilee to Judea, to the city of David called Bethlehem, because he was descended from the house and family of David. He went to be registered with Mary, to whom he was engaged and who was expecting a child. While they were there, the time came for her to deliver her child. And she gave birth to her firstborn son and wrapped him in bands of cloth, and laid him in a manger, because there was no place for them in the inn.

Luke 2:1–7

THE TWELVE
DAYS OF
CHRISTMAS
AND EPIPHANY

Living by God's Mercy

We cannot approach the manger of the Christ child in the same way we approach the cradle of another child. Rather, when we go to his manger, something happens, and we cannot leave it again unless we have been judged or redeemed. Here we must either collapse or know the mercy of God directed toward us.

What does that mean? Isn't all of this just a way of speaking? Isn't it just pastoral exaggeration of a pretty and pious legend? What does it mean that such things are said about the Christ child? Those who want to take it as a way of speaking will do so and continue to celebrate Advent and Christmas as before, with pagan indifference. For us it is not just a way of speaking. For that's just it: it is God himself, the Lord and Creator of all things, who is so small here, who is hidden here in the corner, who enters into the plainness of the world, who meets us in the helplessness and defenselessness of a child, and wants to be with us. And he does this not out of playfulness or sport, because we find that so touching, but in order to show us where he is and who he is, and in order from this place to judge and devalue and dethrone all human ambition.

The throne of God in the world is not on human thrones, but in human depths, in the manger. Standing around his throne there are no flattering vassals but dark, unknown, questionable figures who cannot get their fill of this miracle and want to live entirely by the mercy of God.

❖   ❖   ❖

"Joy to the world!" Anyone for whom this sound is foreign, or who hears in it nothing but weak enthusiasm, has not yet really heard the gospel. For the sake of humankind, Jesus Christ became a human being in a stable in Bethlehem: Rejoice, O Christendom! For sinners, Jesus Christ became a companion of tax collectors and prostitutes: Rejoice, O Christendom! For the condemned, Jesus Christ was condemned to the cross on Golgotha: Rejoice, O Christendom! For all of us, Jesus Christ was resurrected to life: Rejoice, O Christendom! . . . All over the world today people are asking: Where is the path to joy? The church of Christ answers loudly: Jesus is our joy! (1 Pet. 1:7–9). Joy to the world!

Dietrich Bonhoeffer

❖   ❖   ❖

In this you rejoice, even if now for a little while you have had to suffer various trials, so that the genuineness of your faith—being more precious than gold that, though perishable, is tested by fire—may be found to result in praise and glory and honor when Jesus Christ is revealed. Although you have not seen him, you love him; and even though you do not see him now, you believe in him and rejoice with an indescribable and glorious joy, for you are receiving the outcome of your faith, the salvation of your souls.

1 Peter 1:6–9

The Great Kingdom of Peace Has Begun

The authority of this poor child will grow (Isa. 9:7). It will encompass all the earth, and knowingly or unknowingly, all human generations until the end of the ages will have to serve it. It will be an authority over the hearts of people, but thrones and great kingdoms will also grow strong or fall apart with this power. The mysterious, invisible authority of the divine child over human hearts is more solidly grounded than the visible and resplendent power of earthly rulers. Ultimately all authority on earth must serve only the authority of Jesus Christ over humankind.

With the birth of Jesus, the great kingdom of peace has begun. Is it not a miracle that where Jesus has really become Lord over people, peace reigns? That there is one Christendom on the whole earth, in which there is peace in the midst of the world? Only where Jesus is not allowed to reign—where human stubbornness, defiance, hate, and avarice are allowed to live on unbroken—can there be no peace. Jesus does not want to set up his kingdom of peace by force, but where people willingly submit themselves to him and let him rule over them, he will give them his wonderful peace.

❖ ❖ ❖

I'm in the dark depths of night, and my thoughts are roaming far afield. Now that all the merry-making and rejoicing and candlelight are over and the noise and commotion of the day have been replaced by silence, inside and out, other voices can be heard. . . . The chill night wind and the mysterious darkness can open hearts and release forces that are unfathomable, but good and consoling. . . . Can you think of a better time than night-time? That's why Christ, too, chose to come to us — with his angels — at night.[1]

Maria von Wedemeyer to Bonhoeffer,
December 25, 1943

❖   ❖   ❖

Now the birth of Jesus the Messiah took place in this way. When his mother Mary had been engaged to Joseph, but before they lived together, she was found to be with child from the Holy Spirit. Her husband Joseph, being a righteous man and unwilling to expose her to public disgrace, planned to dismiss her quietly. But just when he had resolved to do this, an angel of the Lord appeared to him in a dream and said, "Joseph, son of David, do not be afraid to take Mary as your wife, for the child conceived in her is from the Holy Spirit. She will bear a son, and you are to name him Jesus, for he will save his people from their sins." All this took place to fulfill what had been spoken by the Lord through the prophet:

> "Look, the virgin shall conceive and bear a son,
>   and they shall name him Emmanuel,"

which means, "God is with us." When Joseph awoke from sleep, he did as the angel of the Lord commanded him; he took her as his wife, but had no marital relations with her until she had borne a son; and he named him Jesus.

Matthew 1:18–25

On the Weak Shoulders of a Child

Authority rests upon his shoulders" (Isa. 9:6). Authority over the world is supposed to lie on the weak shoulders of this newborn child! One thing we know: these shoulders will come to carry the entire burden of the world. With the cross, all the sin and distress of this world will be loaded on these shoulders. But authority consists in the fact that the bearer does not collapse under the burden but carries it to the end. The authority that lies on the shoulders of the child in the manger consists in the patient bearing of people and their guilt. This bearing, however, begins in the manger; it begins where the eternal word of God assumes and bears human flesh. The authority over all the world has its beginning in the very lowliness and weakness of the child. . . . He accepts and carries the humble, the lowly, and sinners, but he rejects and brings to nothing the proud, the haughty, and the righteous (Luke 1:51–52).

❖　❖　❖

From the Christian point of view there is no special problem about Christmas in a prison cell. For many people in this building it will probably be a more sincere and genuine occasion than in places where nothing but the name is kept. The misery, suffering, poverty, loneliness, helplessness, and guilt mean something quite different in the eyes of God from what they mean in the judgment of man, that

God will approach where men turn away, that Christ was born in a stable because there was no room for him in the inn—these are things that a prisoner can understand better than other people; for him they really are glad tidings.[2]

Bonhoeffer's letter to his parents from
Tegel prison, December 17, 1943

❖ ❖ ❖

Let the same mind be in you that was in Christ Jesus,
   who, though he was in the form of God,
      did not regard equality with God
      as something to be exploited,
   but emptied himself,
      taking the form of a slave,
      being born in human likeness.
   And being found in human form,
      he humbled himself
      and became obedient to the point of death—
      even death on a cross.

Therefore God also highly exalted him
   and gave him the name
   that is above every name,
   so that at the name of Jesus
      every knee should bend,
      in heaven and on earth and under the earth,
   and every tongue should confess
      that Jesus Christ is Lord,
      to the glory of God the Father.

Philippians 2:5–11

With God There Is Joy

"Everlasting joy shall be upon their heads" (Isa. 35:10). Since ancient times, in the Christian church, acedia—sadness of heart, resignation—has been considered a mortal sin. "Serve the LORD with gladness!" (Ps. 100:2 RSV), urges the Scripture. For this, our life has been given to us, and for this, it has been sustained for us to this present hour. The joy that no one can take from us belongs not only to those who have been called home, but also to us who are still living. In this joy we are one with them, but never in sadness. How are we supposed to be able to help those who are without joy and courage, if we ourselves are not borne by courage and joy? What is meant here is not something made or forced, but something given and free. With God there is joy, and from him it comes down and seizes spirit, soul, and body. And where this joy has seized a person, it reaches out around itself, it pulls others along, it bursts through closed doors. There is a kind of joy that knows nothing at all of the pain, distress, and anxiety of the heart. But it cannot last; it can only numb for a time. The joy of God has gone through the poverty of the manger and the distress of the cross; therefore it is invincible and irrefutable.

❖   ❖   ❖

Acedia may be an unfamiliar term to those not well versed in monastic history or medieval literature. But that does not mean it has no relevance for contemporary readers. . . . I believe that such standard dictionary definitions of *acedia* as "apathy," "boredom," or "torpor" do not begin to cover it, and while we may find it convenient to regard it as a more primitive word for what we now term depression, the truth is much more complex. Having experienced both conditions, I think it likely that most of the restless boredom, frantic escapism, commitment phobia, and enervating despair that plagues us today is the ancient demon of acedia in modern dress.[3]

Kathleen Norris, *Acedia & Me: A Marriage,*
Monks, and a Writer's Life

❖   ❖   ❖

Make a joyful noise to the LORD, all the earth.
　Worship the LORD with gladness;
　come into his presence with singing.

Know that the LORD is God.
　It is he that made us, and we are his;
　we are his people, and the sheep of his pasture.

Enter his gates with thanksgiving,
　and his courts with praise.
　Give thanks to him, bless his name.

For the LORD is good;
　his steadfast love endures forever,
　and his faithfulness to all generations.

Psalm 100

Everlasting Father and Prince of Peace

Everlasting Father" (Isa. 9:6)—how can this be the name of the child? Only because in this child the everlasting fatherly love of God is revealed, and the child wants nothing other than to bring to earth the love of the Father. So the Son is one with the Father, and whoever sees the Son sees the Father. This child wants nothing for himself. He is no prodigy in the human sense, but an obedient child of his heavenly Father. Born in time, he brings eternity with him to earth; as Son of God he brings to us all the love of the Father in heaven. Go, seek, and find in the manger the heavenly Father who here has also become your dear Father.

"Prince of Peace"—where God comes in love to human beings and unites with them, there peace is made between God and humankind and among people. Are you afraid of God's wrath? Then go to the child in the manger and receive there the peace of God. Have you fallen into strife and hatred with your sister or brother? Come and see how God, out of pure love, has become our brother and wants to reconcile us with each other. In the world, power reigns. This child is the Prince of Peace. Where he is, peace reigns.

❖　❖　❖

In our lives we don't speak readily of victory. It is too big a word for us. We have suffered too many defeats in our lives; victory has been thwarted again and again by too many weak hours, too many gross sins. But isn't it true that the spirit within us yearns for this word, for the final victory over the sin and anxious fear of death in our lives? And now God's word also says nothing to us about our victory; it doesn't promise us that *we* will be victorious over sin and death from now own; rather, it says with all its might that someone has won this victory, and that this person, if we have him as Lord, will also win the victory over us. It is not we who are victorious, but Jesus.[4]

"Christus Victor" address, November 26, 1939

❖ ❖ ❖

On that day, when evening had come, he said to them, "Let us go across to the other side." And leaving the crowd behind, they took him with them in the boat, just as he was. Other boats were with him. A great windstorm arose, and the waves beat into the boat, so that the boat was already being swamped. But he was in the stern, asleep on the cushion; and they woke him up and said to him, "Teacher, do you not care that we are perishing?" He woke up and rebuked the wind, and said to the sea, "Peace! Be still!" Then the wind ceased, and there was a dead calm. He said to them, "Why are you afraid? Have you still no faith?" And they were filled with great awe and said to one another, "Who then is this, that even the wind and the sea obey him?"

Mark 4:35–41

Beside Your Cradle Here I Stand

A verse is going around repeatedly in my head:
"Brother, come; from all that grieves you / you
are freed; / all you need / I again will bring you." What
does this mean: "All you need I again will bring you"?
Nothing is lost; in Christ everything is lifted up, pre-
served—to be sure, in a different form—transparent,
clear, freed from the torment of self-seeking desire.
Christ will bring all of this again, and as it was originally intended by God, without the distortion caused
by our sin. The teaching of the gathering up of all
things, found in Ephesians 1:10, is a wonderful and
thoroughly comforting idea. "God seeks out what
has gone by" (Eccl. 3:15) receives here its fulfillment.
And no one has expressed that as simply and in such
a childlike way as Paul Gerhardt in the words that
he places in the mouth of the Christ child: "All you
need I again will bring you." Moreover, for the first
time in these days I have discovered for myself the
song, "Beside your cradle here I stand." Until now I
had not thought much about it. Apparently you have
to be alone a long time and read it meditatively to be
able to perceive it. . . . Beside the "we" there is also
still an "I" and Christ, and what that means cannot be
said better than in this song.

❖   ❖   ❖

When God's Son took on flesh, he truly and bodily took on, out of pure grace, our being, our nature, ourselves. This was the eternal counsel of the triune God. Now we are in him. Where he is, there we are too, in the incarnation, on the cross, and in his resurrection. We belong to him because we are in him. That is why the Scriptures call us the Body of Christ.[5]

Dietrich Bonhoeffer

❖   ❖   ❖

With all wisdom and insight he has made known to us the mystery of his will, according to his good pleasure that he set forth in Christ, as a plan for the fullness of time, to gather up all things in him, things in heaven and things on earth. In Christ we have also obtained an inheritance, having been destined according to the purpose of him who accomplishes all things according to his counsel and will, so that we, who were the first to set our hope on Christ, might live for the praise of his glory.

Ephesians 1:8b–12

The Joyous Certainty of Faith

On the basis of God's beginning with us, which has already happened, our life with God is a path that is traveled in the law of God. Is this human enslavement under the law? No, it is liberation from the murderous law of incessant beginnings. Waiting day after day for the new beginning, thinking countless times that we have found it, only in the evening to give up on it again as lost—that is the perfect destruction of faith in the God who set the beginning once and for all time. . . . God has set the beginning: this is the joyous certainty of faith. Therefore, beside the "one" beginning of God, I am not supposed to try to set countless other beginnings of my own. This is precisely what I am now liberated from. The beginning—God's beginning—lies behind me, once and for all time. . . . Together we are on the path whose beginning consists in the fact that God has found his own people, a path whose end can consist only in the fact that God is seeking us again. The path between this beginning and this end is our walk in the law of God. It is life under the word of God in all its many facets. In truth there is only one danger on this path, namely, wanting to go behind the beginning. In that moment the path stops being a way of grace and faith. It stops being God's own way.

❖ ❖ ❖

I believe that God can and will bring good out of evil, even out of the greatest evil. For that purpose he needs men who make the best use of everything. I believe that God will give us all the strength we need to help us to resist in all times of distress. But he never gives it in advance, lest we should rely on ourselves and not on him alone. A faith such as this should allay all our fears for the future. I believe that even our mistakes and shortcomings are turned to good account, and that it is no harder for God to deal with them than with our supposedly good deeds. I believe that God is no timeless fate, but that he waits for and answers sincere prayers and responsible actions.[6]

"After Ten Years: A Reckoning Made
at New Year 1943"

❖ ❖ ❖

We know that all things work together for good for those who love God, who are called according to his purpose. For those whom he foreknew he also pre-destined to be conformed to the image of his Son, in order that he might be the firstborn within a large family. And those whom he predestined he also called; and those whom he called he also justified; and those whom he justified he also glorified.

Romans 8:28–30

At the Beginning of a New Year

The road to hell is paved with good intentions." This saying, which is found in a broad variety of lands, does not arise from the brash worldly wisdom of an incorrigible. It instead reveals deep Christian insight. At the beginning of a new year, many people have nothing better to do than to make a list of bad deeds and resolve from now on—how many such "from-now-ons" have there already been!—to begin with better intentions, but they are still stuck in the middle of their paganism. They believe that a good intention already means a new beginning; they believe that on their own they can make a new start whenever they want. But that is an evil illusion: only God can make a new beginning with people whenever God pleases, but not people with God. Therefore, people cannot make a new beginning at all; they can only pray for one. Where people are on their own and live by their own devices, there is only the old, the past. Only where God is can there be a new beginning. We cannot command God to grant it; we can only pray to God for it. And we can pray only when we realize that we cannot do anything, that we have reached our limit, that someone else must make that new beginning.

❖   ❖   ❖

New Year's Text:

If we survive during the coming weeks or months, we shall be able to see quite clearly that all has turned out for the best. The idea that we could have avoided many of life's difficulties if we had taken things more cautiously is too foolish to be entertained for a moment. As I look back on your past I am so convinced that what has happened hitherto has been right, that I feel that what is happening now is right too. To renounce a full life and its real joys in order to avoid pain is neither Christian nor human.[7]

Bonhoeffer to Renate and Eberhard Bethge, written from Tegel, January 23, 1944

❖   ❖   ❖

From now on, therefore, we regard no one from a human point of view; even though we once knew Christ from a human point of view, we know him no longer in that way. So if anyone is in Christ, there is a new creation: everything old has passed away; see, everything has become new!

2 Corinthians 5:16–17

⁓ ⁓

Do Not Worry about Tomorrow

Possessions delude the human heart into believing that they provide security and a worry-free existence, but in truth they are the very cause of worry. For the heart that is fixed on possessions, they come with a suffocating burden of worry. Worries lead to treasure, and treasure leads back to worry. We want to secure our lives through possessions; through worry we want to become worry free, but the truth turns out to be the opposite. The shackles that bind us to possessions, that hold us fast to possessions, are themselves worries. The misuse of possessions consists in our using them for security for the next day. Worry is always directed toward tomorrow. In the strictest sense, however, possessions are intended only for today. It is precisely the securing of tomorrow that makes me so insecure today. "Today's trouble is enough for today" (Matt. 6:34b). Only those who place tomorrow in God's hands and receive what they need to live today are truly secure. Receiving daily liberates us from tomorrow. Thought for tomorrow delivers us up to endless worry.

❖ ❖ ❖

I have had the experience over and over again that the quieter it is around me, the clearer do I feel the connection to you. It is as though in solitude the soul develops senses which we hardly know in everyday life. Therefore I have not felt lonely or abandoned for one moment. You, the parents, all of you, the friends and students of mine at the front, all are constantly present to me. . . . Therefore you must not think me unhappy. What is happiness and unhappiness? It depends so little on the circumstances; it depends really only on that which happens inside a person.[8]

Bonhoeffer's final Christmastime letter to fiancée
Maria von Wedemeyer, December 19, 1944

❖   ❖   ❖

"Therefore do not worry, saying, 'What will we eat?' or 'What will we drink?' or 'What will we wear?' For it is the Gentiles who strive for all these things; and indeed your heavenly Father knows that you need all these things. But strive first for the kingdom of God and his righteousness, and all these things will be given to you as well.

"So do not worry about tomorrow, for tomorrow will bring worries of its own. Today's trouble is enough for today."

Matthew 6:31–34

A Necessary Daily Exercise

Why is it that my thoughts wander so quickly from God's word, and that in my hour of need the needed word is often not there? Do I forget to eat and drink and sleep? Then why do I forget God's word? Because I still can't say what the psalmist says: "I will delight in your statutes" (Ps. 119:16). I don't forget the things in which I take delight. Forgetting or not forgetting is a matter not of the mind but of the whole person, of the heart. I never forget what body and soul depend upon. The more I begin to love the commandments of God in creation and word, the more present they will be for me in every hour. Only love protects against forgetting.

Because God's word has spoken to us in history and thus in the past, the remembrance and repetition of what we have learned is a necessary daily exercise. Every day we must turn again to God's acts of salvation, so that we can again move forward. . . . Faith and obedience live on remembrance and repetition. Remembrance becomes the power of the present because of the living God who once acted for me and who reminds me of that today.

❖ ❖ ❖

In our meditation we ponder the chosen text on the strength of the promise that it has something utterly personal to say to us for this day and for our Christian life, that it is not only God's word for the Church, but also God's word for us individually. We expose ourselves to the specific word until it addresses us personally. And when we do this, we are doing no more than the simplest, untutored Christian does every day; we read God's word as God's word for us.[9]

Bonhoeffer, *Life Together*

❖ ❖ ❖

I treasure your word in my heart,
     so that I may not sin against you.
Blessed are you, O LORD;
     teach me your statutes.
With my lips I declare
     all the ordinances of your mouth.
I delight in the way of your decrees
     as much as in all riches.
I will meditate on your precepts,
     and fix my eyes on your ways.
I will delight in your statutes;
     I will not forget your word.

Deal bountifully with your servant,
     so that I may live and observe your word.
Open my eyes, so that I may behold
     wondrous things out of your law.

Psalm 119:11–18

For Everything There Is a Season

For those who find and give thanks to God in their earthly fortune, God will give them times in which to remember that all things on earth are only temporary, and that it is good to set one's heart on eternity. . . . All things have their time, and the main thing is to stay in step with God and not always be hurrying a few steps ahead or falling behind. To want everything all at once is to be overanxious. "For everything there is a season . . . to weep, and . . . to laugh; . . . to embrace, and . . . to refrain from embracing; . . . to tear, and . . . to sew . . ." (Eccl. 3:1a, 4a, 5b, 7a), "and God seeks out what has gone by" (3:15b). Yet this last part must mean that nothing past is lost, that with us God again seeks out the past that belongs to us. So when the longing for something past overtakes us—and this happens at completely unpredictable times—then we can know that this is only one of the many "times" that God makes available to us. And then we should not proceed on our own but seek out the past once again with God.

❖　❖　❖

Dear Mother, I want you to know that I am constantly thinking of you and Father every day, and that I thank God for all that you are to me and the whole family. I know you've always lived for us and haven't lived a life of your own. . . . Thank you for all the love that has come to me in my cell from you during the past year, and has made every day easier for me. I think these hard years have brought us closer together than ever we were before. My wish for you and Father and Maria and for us all is that the New Year may bring us at least an occasional glimmer of light, and that we may once more have the opportunity of being together. May God keep you both well.[10]

Birthday letter to Bonhoeffer's mother
from prison, December 28, 1944

❖   ❖   ❖

For everything there is a season, and a time for every matter under heaven:
    a time to be born, and a time to die;
    a time to plant, and a time to pluck up what is
        planted;
    a time to kill, and a time to heal;
    a time to break down, and a time to build up;
    a time to weep, and a time to laugh;
    a time to mourn, and a time to dance;
    a time to throw away stones, and a time to
        gather stones together;
    a time to embrace, and a time to refrain from
        embracing;
    a time to seek, and a time to lose;
    a time to keep, and a time to throw away;
    a time to tear, and a time to sew;
    a time to keep silence, and a time to speak;
    a time to love, and a time to hate;
    a time for war, and a time for peace.

Ecclesiastes 3:1–8

Morning by Morning He Wakens Me

Every new morning is a new beginning of our life. Every day is a completed whole. The present day should be the boundary of our care and striving (Matt. 6:34; Jas. 4:14). It is long enough for us to find God or lose God, to keep the faith or fall into sin and shame. God created day and night so that we might not wander boundlessly, but already in the morning may see the goal of the evening before us. As the old sun rises new every day, so the eternal mercies of God are new every morning (Lam. 3:22–23). To grasp the old faithfulness of God anew every morning, to be able — in the middle of life — to begin a new life with God daily, that is the gift that God gives with every new morning. . . .

Not fear of the day, not the burden of work that I have to do, but rather, the Lord wakens me. So says the servant of God: "Morning by morning he wakens — wakens my ear to listen as those who are taught" (Isa. 50:4c). God wants to open the heart before it opens itself to the world; before the ear hears the innumerable voices of the day, the early hours are the time to hear the voice of the Creator and Redeemer. God made the stillness of the early morning for himself. It ought to belong to God.

❖ ❖ ❖

Because intercession is such an incalculably great gift of God, we should accept it joyfully. The very time we give to intercession will turn out to be a daily source of new joy in God and in the Christian community. . . . For most people the early morning will prove to be the best time. We have a right to this time, even prior to the claims of other people, and we may insist upon having it as a completely undisturbed quiet time despite all external difficulties.[11]

Bonhoeffer, *Life Together*

❖ ❖ ❖

The Lord GOD has given me
the tongue of a teacher,
that I may know how to sustain
the weary with a word.
Morning by morning he wakens—
wakens my ear
to listen as those who are taught.

Isaiah 50:4

The Feast of Epiphany

The curious uncertainty that surrounds the feast of Epiphany is as old as the feast itself. We know that long before Christmas was celebrated, Epiphany was the highest holiday in the Eastern and Western churches. Its origins are obscure, but it is certain that since ancient times this day has brought to mind four different events: the birth of Christ, the baptism of Christ, the wedding at Cana, and the arrival of the Magi from the East. . . . Be that as it may, since the fourth century the church has left the birth of Christ out of the feast of Epiphany. . . . The removal of the birth of Christ from his baptismal day had great significance. In gnostic and heretical circles in the East, the idea arose that the baptismal day was actually the day of Christ's birth as the Son of God. . . . But therein lay the possibility of a dangerous error, namely, a misunderstanding of God's incarnation. . . . If God had not accepted Jesus as his Son until Jesus' baptism, we would remain unredeemed. But if Jesus is the Son of God who from his conception and birth assumed our own flesh and blood, then and then alone is he true man and true God; only then can he help us; for then the "hour of salvation" for us has really come in his birth; then the birth of Christ is the salvation of all people.

❖　❖　❖

Today you will be baptized a Christian. All those great ancient words of the Christian proclamation will be spoken over you, and the command of Jesus Christ to baptize will be carried out on you, without your knowing anything about it. But we are once again being driven right back to the beginnings of our understanding. Reconciliation and redemption, regeneration and the Holy Spirit, love of our enemies, cross and resurrection, life in Christ and Christian discipleship.[12]

"Thoughts on the Baptism of
Dietrich Wilhelm Rüdiger Bethge,"
May 1944

❖   ❖   ❖

When they had heard the king, they set out; and there, ahead of them, went the star that they had seen at its rising, until it stopped over the place where the child was. When they saw that the star had stopped, they were overwhelmed with joy. On entering the house, they saw the child with Mary his mother; and they knelt down and paid him homage. Then, opening their treasure chests, they offered him gifts of gold, frankincense, and myrrh. And having been warned in a dream not to return to Herod, they left for their own country by another road.

Matthew 2:9–12

NOTES

Editor's Preface

1. Stephen R. Haynes and Lori Brandt Hale, *Bonhoeffer for Armchair Theologians* (Louisville, Ky.: Westminster John Knox Press, 2009). See esp. 132–33 and 77–78.

2. Eberhard Bethge, *Dietrich Bonhoeffer: A Biography*, rev. ed. (Minneapolis: Fortress Press, 2000), 260.

3. Letter from Dietrich Bonhoeffer to Eberhard Bethge, November 21, 1943, in *Letters and Papers from Prison: New Greatly Enlarged Edition*, ed. Eberhard Bethge (New York: Touchstone, 1997), 135.

4. Haynes and Hale, *Bonhoeffer for Armchair Theologians*, 70–76.

Advent Week One: Waiting

1. Dietrich Bonhoeffer, *Dietrich Bonhoeffer's Christmas Sermons*, ed. and trans. Edwin Robertson (Grand Rapids: Zondervan, 2005), 171–72.

2. Ruth-Alice von Bismarck and Ulrich Kabitz, *Love Letters from Cell 92: The Correspondence between Dietrich Bonhoeffer and Maria von Wedemeyer, 1943–45* (Nashville: Abingdon Press, 1992), 133.

3. *Ibid.*, 128.

4. Dietrich Bonhoeffer, "The Coming of Jesus in Our Midst," in *Watch for the Light: Readings for Advent and Christmas* (Maryknoll, N.Y.: Orbis Books, 2001), 205.

5. Dietrich Bonhoeffer, *I Want to Live These Days with You* (Louisville, Ky.: Westminster John Knox Press, 2007), 369.

6. Bonhoeffer, *Letters and Papers from Prison*, 135.

7. Bonhoeffer, *I Want to Live These Days with You*, 366.

Advent Week Two: Mystery

1. Bonhoeffer, *I Want to Live These Days with You*, 152.

2. Bismarck and Kabitz, *Love Letters from Cell 92*, 138.

3. Bonhoeffer, *I Want to Live These Days with You*, 149.

4. Brennan Manning, *The Ragamuffin Gospel Visual Edition* (Sisters, Ore.: Multnomah Publishers, 2005), n.p.

5. Bonhoeffer, *I Want to Live These Days with You*, 377.

6. Eugene Peterson, "Introduction," in *God with Us: Rediscovering the Meaning of Christmas*, ed. Greg Pennoyer and Gregory Wolfe (Brewster, Mass.: Paraclete Press, 2007), 1.

7. Scott Cairns, in *God with Us*, 57.

Advent Week Three: Redemption

1. Dietrich Bonhoeffer, *A Testament to Freedom: The Essential Writings of Dietrich Bonhoeffer*, ed. Geffrey B. Kelly and F. Burton Nelson (San Francisco: HarperOne, 1990, 1995), 217.

2. Bonhoeffer, *Dietrich Bonhoeffer's Christmas Sermons*, 22–23.

3. Ibid., 103–4.

4. Bonhoeffer, *Testament to Freedom*, 223.

5. Bonhoeffer, *Letters and Papers from Prison*, 323.

6. Bonhoeffer, *Testament to Freedom*, 185–86.

7. Ibid., 218.

Advent Week Four: Incarnation

1. Bonhoeffer, *Dietrich Bonhoeffer's Christmas Sermons*, 151. By Christmas of 1940, the Nazis had forbidden Bonhoeffer to preach publicly. This excerpt comes from a Christmas sermon he wrote that was circulated in print.

2. Frederica Mathewes-Green, *At the Corner of East and Now: A Modern Life in Ancient Christian Orthodoxy* (New York: Penguin Putnam, 1999), posted online at http://www.frederica.com/east-now-excerpt-1/.

3. Bonhoeffer, *Dietrich Bonhoeffer's Christmas Sermons*, 38–39.

4. Ibid., 151–52.

5. Ibid., 37.

6. Luci Shaw, in *God with Us*, 77–78.

7. Bismarck and Kabitz, *Love Letters from Cell 92*, 132.

The Twelve Days of Christmas

1. Bismarck and Kabitz, *Love Letters from Cell 92*, 145.

2. Bonhoeffer, *Letters and Papers from Prison*, 166.

3. Kathleen Norris, *Acedia & Me: A Marriage, Monks, and a Writer's Life* (New York: Riverhead, 2008), 2–3.

4. In *Dietrich Bonhoeffer: Writings Selected with an Introduction by Robert Coles* (Maryknoll, N.Y.: Orbis Books, 1998), 88.

5. Dietrich Bonhoeffer, *Life Together: The Classic Exploration of Christian Community* (New York: Harper, 1954), 24.

6. In *Dietrich Bonhoeffer: Writings*, 111–12. This New Year's reflection was written by Bonhoeffer in 1943 and circulated in a small way among his friends and coconspirators against Hitler, but it was not published until after his death.

7. Bonhoeffer, *Letters and Papers from Prison*, 191.

8. Ibid., 419.

9. Bonhoeffer, *Life Together*, 82.

10. In *Dietrich Bonhoeffer: Writings*, 126–27.

11. Bonhoeffer, *Life Together*, 87.

12. Bonhoeffer, *Testament to Freedom*, 504–5.

SCRIPTURE INDEX

CPSIA information can be obtained
at www.ICGtesting.com
Printed in the USA
FSOW01n0859101115
13197FS